BERLIN YESTERDAY

Published by GINGKO PRESS Inc.
5768 Paradise Drive, Suite J, Corte Madera, CA 94925, USA
Phone (415) 924-9615, Fax (415) 924-9608
email Gingko@linex.com
Copyright © English Edition 1998

3-927258-70-9

"So war Berlin"
First published 1997 by Kunstverlag Weingarten, Germany
Copyright © 1997 Kunstverlag Weingarten GmbH

← The "Emperor's Passage", the center section of the Brandenburg Gate, was not open to public traffic until 1927

BERLIN

YESTERDAY

Gingko Press
Corte Madera, California
1998

View down Scharrenstraße to Petri Chrurch

INTRODUCTION

Every European city has its famous land-marks. Rome has St. Peters, Paris has the Eiffel Tower, and London, of course, has its Tower. These cities are thousands of years old, and they have many buildings which are evidence of their passage through time. Churches, palaces, in some cases entire streets and neighbourhoods reflect the architectural and urban changes that have occurred over many centuries.

Not so Berlin! Although it is also several hundred years old, Berlin remained com-paratively insignificant until the end of the 19th century. In fact it was not until 1880 that Berlin's development began in earnest, a turbulent, dynamic develop-ment that was to surpass even that of American cities.

It was within only a few decades that the relatively modest German capital evolved into the metropolitan city we know today, and it was during this time that most of Berlin's old buildings were torn down and replaced. Scrutinised closely, Berlin actu-ally looks like a city that grew quickly, pre-senting a degree of architectural uniformity that is largely lacking in Europe's other major metropolitan centers.

For most other cities the whole of the 19th century was a period of constant change - change that was primarily driven by de-velopments in transportation and the es-tablishment of manufacturing plants. With the new means of transport came the need for wider streets and roads which demand-ed radical structural change. The builders of the day tended to focus on the existing 'framework' or grid; but new construction often resulted in the erection of buildings of previously unheard of dimensions.

In Berlin, though, change was limited to specific areas which is why its appearance was never entirely transformed. Berlin was able to self confidently maintain the homogeneous appearance of a city with few historical relics.

The photos presented here were taken during the 1920s and early 1930s. They document the changes taking place in the city and present an image of Berlin as seen through the eye of the camera. Gone are the representative panoramic shots of the most important streets and squares, as taken by Waldemar Tietzenthaler and Max Missmann. And there is little evidence of the "Zille Milieu", which was then considered so characteristic of Berlin. Instead, these are photos that concisely describe a condition: they report on objects of interest with little concern for details. These are not postcard pictures, but illustrations for everyday journalism.

The purpose determines the subject: natural phenomena and their effects, economic events such as strikes or sales, indications of new construction such as modern apartment complexes, swimming pools and department stores. All point to economic and social changes taking place within the city, thus documenting the distinctly new urban climate of that time.

Some photographs attempt to capture the atmosphere of Berlin during the late 19th century. They portray the suggestive power of the Wilhelminian capital and help us to understand why this power, even today, remains unbroken.

Through these images it is clear to see that even though many of Berlin's most important buildings have since been destroyed, Berlin's vitality, dynamism and flair will have a lasting influence on our powers of imagination for a long time to come.

Berlin in the 20s was a mixture of the traditional with just a few modern elements. In this respect it very much resembled the Weimar Republic, of which it was the capital.

Christian Wolsdorff

↑ Kreuzstrasse with its 17th and 18th century buildings

← View of the Lange Brücke from the Elector's corner room in Berlin Castle

↑ Children playing in Old Berlin

→ Dancing in an inner courtyard

Erster-Hof.
Bade-
Anstalt
Holz-Kohlen
&
Kartoffelhandlung
nächster Hof.

↑ Small Traders at Bülowplatz →

← Inner courtyards are typical of Berlin's apartment blocks. Meyer's courtyard in Wedding is pictured here

The pub "Dom-Klause" on the ground floor of the Russian Church on Hohenzollerndamm in Berlin Wilmersdorf

↑ Potsdamer Platz was Europe's busiest square in the late 1920s → Postdamer Platz

Rear view of Bismarck Memorial in front of the Reichstag with view of the Victory Column

Brandenburg Gate, west side facing the Tiergarten

↑ Unter den Linden, seen from Brandenburg Gate.   → Subway construction at Alexander Platz (1927-30)

↑ Gerson clothing store at Werdersche Market. In the background: Friedrichswerder Church, built by Karl Friedrich Schinkel

← Grenadierstrasse in the suburb of Spandau

Alsenbridge and the old harbor

Tugboat Harbor at Spandauer Bridge

↑ Harbour at Lehrter Train Station, where a large volume of freight passes through every day

→ Fruit and vegatables grown outside Berlin are brought into the city on the Spree riverboats. They get sold directly from the deck, as seen at the stock exchange

Mühlendamm Lock in the center of Berlin

A floating grocer supplies boatmen on the Spree

Tiergarten Lock

↑ Waisenbrücke at the Märkische Museum

→ The annual parade of Spree steamers opens the boating season. In the background the cathedral

Narrow alleys in Old Berlin, of which very few still existed in the late 1920s

Subway construction at St. George's Church

↑ Tietz Department Store at Alexanderplatz

← Tietz Department Store on the Leipziger Strasse

In front of Rudolph & Rudolph Leather Shop on the Leipziger Strasse

↑ The first department store in Berlin with street sales in Berlin Tempelhof

→ The busy Central Market on Neue Friedrichstrasse at 6 a.m.

↑ Shopping by motorcycle (posed)

← Selling firewood at Schlossbrücke in Berlin Charlottenburg

52

Card game among market workers (posed)

Advertising for Tilsit cheese at Potsdamer Platz

Shoe shiner at Unter den Linden

Lamp cleaner in front of the Shell Building

Chimney sweep – father and son

↑ Advertising Parade on Kaiserdamm

← Berlin Hauler's Guild demonstration with more than 1,000 motorized and horse-drawn vehicles in the Lust-garten (1930)

→ Striking hackney drivers (1930)

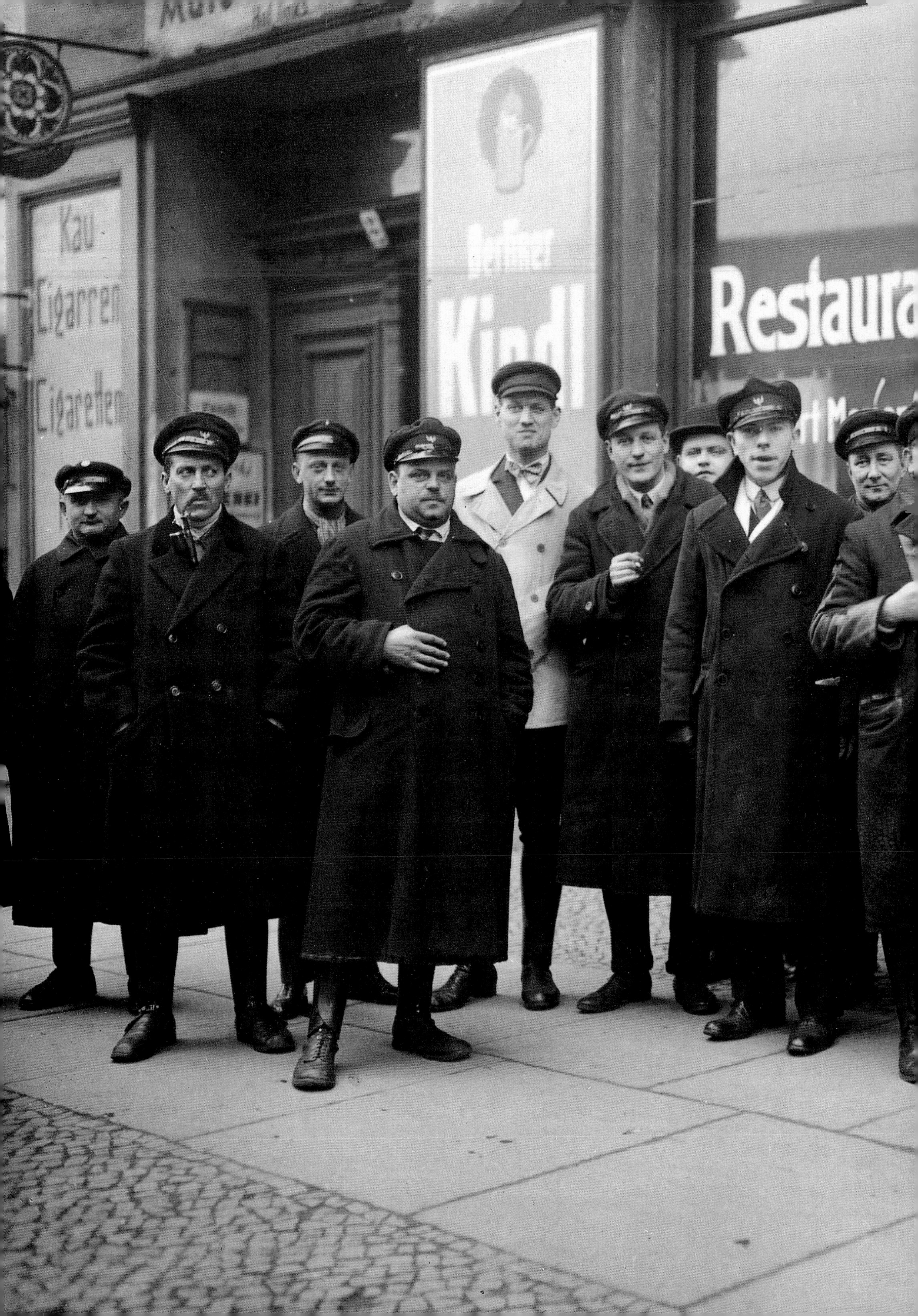
Kau
Cigarren
Cigaretten
Berliner
Kindl
Restaura

↑ Crowd at the ice cream parlor on "Children's Day", when ice cream is cheaper for children

← New coffee counter at Woolworth's on Bellevuestrasse

Advertising for a bar

Bakery window display with a portrait of President Hindenburg

Advertising column at Hallesches Tor

Newsstand around 1930

↑ Nannies meet at the childrens playground

← "Belphegor – The Riddle of Paris", playing at the Primus Palace on Urbanstrasse in Berlin Kreuzberg

Dance floor at Kroll-Garten